In Honor of Milo Folley

From His Daughter

Brooke Counts

FATHER DAUGHTER

FATHER
DAUGHTER

Photographs by Terry Corrao

Foreword by J.B. White

Colfax Press

Published by Colfax Press
1130 University Boulevard, Suite B9, Box 544
Tuscaloosa, Alabama 35401
www.fatherdaughterthebook.com
www.terrycorrao.com

First Edition

ISBN: 978-0-9973604-0-0

Library of Congress Control Number: 2016954443

Individual text and captions by Terry Corrao, © 2016
Foreword by J.B. White, © 2014
Photographs on page x by Elizabeth White, © 2014
Photographs on page xii from the Stevenson Family Archive, © 2016
All other photographs by Terry Corrao, © 2016

Drawing of Margaret Hamilton in *The Three Sisters*, 1977, by Al Hirschfeld,
© The Al Hirschfeld Foundation, www.AlHirschfeldFoundation.org

Brief quote ["How many more times will you remember a certain afternoon….limitless."]
from THE SHELTERING SKY by PAUL BOWLES, Copyright 1949 by Paul Bowles,
(c) renewed 1977 by Paul Bowles. Reprinted by permission of HarperCollins Publishers.

Editor: Terry Corrao and Angelo Corrao
Book Design: Amanda Shaw
Copy Editor: Emily Conner
Typesetting: Michele Myatt Quinn
Publishing Consultant: Easty Lambert-Brown

60 duotone plates

Printed in Canada

FRONTISPIECE: CARLOS AND ANALIS SOCA
Account Manager & Program Director, Walt Disney World Advertising
Wolcott, Connecticut   1996

Dedicated to my father

for whom the glass was always full.

CONTENTS

J.B., MARY, ISABEL, and EMMA WHITE
Screenwriter
Ojai, California   1994

FOREWORD

It is widely believed every father wants a son and hopes his firstborn will be a boy. That is not true of me. I always suspected I would be ill-suited as a father of sons. I'm not into "guy" things. Except for a disastrous season in second grade Little League (where I had the worst batting average in the league), I have never played sports and rarely watch them. My wife Elizabeth is far handier with tools than I am, and the one time I tried to put oil in my car, I destroyed the water pump instead. I've always appreciated "girly" things much more: fashion, ballet, romantic movies. Elizabeth and I had struggled for many years to have children, so when we were finally able to, we were overjoyed at the simple prospect of having a *baby*. We had names picked out, and when the time came, in April 1983, it was Emma who emerged, not Owen. Twenty-two months later, it was Mary, not Sam. And three years after that, Isabel, not Abraham. Elizabeth and I knew we were done begetting children, and so all girls it was—and I couldn't have been happier.

Being a father of daughters (and husband to their mother) has been the greatest joy of my life, a daily source of emotional nourishment. I've loved their company at every stage of the journey—even their teenaged years.

None of that "how sharper than a serpent's tooth" stuff for me. When I take stock of my life, something I find myself doing as I get older, my career as a father is something I look upon and say, "I did a pretty good job there." I like to think I've provided my daughters with a positive, workable model of what a man can and should be. I would have felt the same if I'd had sons, but to hope I've done that for our girls (they will always be "our girls") feels like an important accomplishment. I see it most clearly in how they deal with the young men in their lives—the level of respect, honesty and commitment they ask of and need from them. When it's there, the relationships flourish; when it isn't, they're ultimately out the door.

I bet every father of daughters feels that way, which is why I believe the book you're holding is so special. Terry Corrao had an insight into how profound the bond between fathers and daughters is, and she set out to chronicle those relationships in photographs. The tremendous depth and breadth of feeling and connection she has captured in these images take my breath away. I was the first father she photographed, and I consider that a great honor. I'm sure all the fathers featured have a clear memory of how they felt when their photos were taken. I certainly do…

photo by Elizabeth White, 2014

The late winter of 1994, when the photo was taken, was a fraught time in our lives. A few months earlier, believing I could make a living as a screenwriter, I quit my job as a legal secretary in New York City, Elizabeth and I sold our house in New Jersey, and we moved with the girls to Southern California. Not wanting to raise them in L.A., we settled in nearby Ojai. At that point, the dream of a screenwriting career was just that: a dream. Although I had signed with a major talent agency, I had not yet sold a script or been hired to write one. We had enough resources to last a year, but if no work came, what then? We had figuratively jumped off a cliff.

None of this was lost on my daughters. The move was traumatic for them. They loved our home back east. They had friends there and were part of a safe, familiar community. Despite its sunshine, California was unknown and sometimes frightening territory; the air of uncertainty that informed our future was impossible for them to ignore. Shortly after arriving, we were all severely jolted by the Northridge earthquake and its aftershocks. They had every reason to believe we were on shaky ground, which is deeply disconcerting to a child.

When I look at this photo, taken outside our first Ojai home, a rental, I see all of that. Emma's wariness, Mary's guarded smile (she'd just come home from a classmate's birthday party; thus the balloon), Isabel's clear-eyed, somber surrender. And me, eyes closed, facing heavenward, praying that my decision to bring us here had been the right one and not an act of insanity. I can still feel that moment, how I luxuriated in them, drawn close and wrapped around me, relishing what was most important to me then and now— my family, whom I vowed to cherish and protect.

Through good fortune, the dream did come true. Shortly after the photo was taken, I sold my first pitch, and I have been a working screenwriter ever since. Elizabeth and I are still happily married and living in Ojai, and family remains our reason for being. We see the girls frequently (Mary and Isabel live in San Francisco; Emma in Europe with her wonderful French husband) and, in the age of social networking, are in touch with them daily. As I write this, Elizabeth and Emma are in Mallorca. They return in a few days, and the five us will meet in Tahoe for a week, where we will eat, drink, hike, play Pictionary Against Humanity (our own hybrid creation), and revel in the immense pleasure of each other's company. Terry's photo hangs on the wall just outside our bedroom, a constant reminder of how far we've come together. I know the fathers and daughters in every photo here have their own memories and stories related to the moment when Terry captured them on film and, like me, are so grateful that she did.

J. B. WHITE, August 2014

THE STEVENSON FAMILY

INTRODUCTION

It was the winter of 1994 and I was making the two-hour drive home from Riverside County to Los Angeles along Interstate 15, a monotonous landscape that had grown all too familiar. I had just left my father's bedside, where I realized it would probably be the last time we would be together. He had suffered a long illness and the look in his eyes revealed a peaceful acceptance of what was to come. It was an emotional drive home, alone in the car, as I pondered what I was about to lose; images of my childhood with Dad played back like pictures from an old family album.

My father, Charles Stevenson, known to friends and family as Chuck, C. M., and Duke, imbued my life with *joie de vivre.* He adored being the father of three girls, watching us grow up in rural Southern California through the 1950s. He delighted in spending time with us, from early morning horseback rides to chicken fights in the pool, as well as introducing us to the grownup things he loved like steak tartare, card games, and horse races. From an early age I observed that any racehorse that Willie Shoemaker rode was a sure thing. And more than a few nights we spent perfecting blackjack tactics at the dining room table. Once, after overhearing Dad's technique for the perfect martini, I

couldn't wait to share it with my second grade teacher Sister Margaret Mary. (A conference was called.)

My parents were a stunning couple. My father was a city boy from Chicago who joined the Navy after his freshman year at Williams College. Old photos show him to be dashing in his naval uniform. Something of a ladies man in his early years (and perhaps in his later years), he was witty, charming, and optimistic to a fault. During the war, he was stationed at Hyannis on Cape Cod, where he met Judy Gildemeister, a Navy WAVE who was operating the airport control tower where he had been sent to repair the radio. It was love at first sight—even though she outranked him. Mom was a Texan, a San Antonio beauty. She was a superb horsewoman and an aviatrix. They married a year after the war ended and lived in Chicago, where my younger sister and I were born.

In 1951, my grandfather closed the doors to the Chicago family business, the Stevenson Pie Company, and all of us—parents, grandparents, aunts, uncles, my newborn sister, and I—followed the masses escaping frigid Midwest winters to sunny Southern California. Within a couple of years, our youngest sister was born, making us three girls within four years. We were a typical family of that post-war generation, living the dream shared by many during the Eisenhower era. Illustrated magazines like *Life, Look,* and *The Saturday Evening Post* were scattered about the house, and the black and white television was ever-present, always on. Mom and Dad entertained frequently and cocktail parties often commenced at a moment's notice.

Dad worked for Oscar Mayer, often surprising us at our birthday parties with visits from Little Oscar and the Wienermobile, a car shaped like a hotdog on a bun that terrified the horses. Mom was a homemaker, hospital volunteer, and Girl Scout leader. My mother's many accomplishments made an early impression on me and I strove to emulate her by setting my goals to her milestones—leaving home by 20, marrying by 23, having children by 26. With Dad, it was different. He and I had an unspoken code of understanding, that wink shared between best of pals. While Mom bore the burden of being the disciplinarian, Dad was the sympathetic listener to whom I always turned. It gave us a means of standing by each other in times of trouble, both his and mine, and provided the basis for a life-long trust that sustained us through the highs and lows.

By the time I was fifteen, my parents' marriage had grown rocky, and alcohol-fueled arguments clouded the evening air. A painful separation and divorce followed. Whisked away to Texas by our mother, my sisters and I didn't see our father for several years. But Dad and I stayed in each other's lives, exchanging long letters every month. It was four years before my father and I were reunited. We both had new lives; I had followed the flower children to San Francisco in the late 1960s, and he had remarried and started a new career. The moment we saw each other, however, we embraced in bear hugs of love and affection as

tears fell. The unspoken understanding was still there, and we knew everything was going to be all right...although the braless hippie look was a bit much for him.

Several years later, I met my husband, a feature film editor based in New York. We married and had two children—a son and a daughter, on whom I perpetually turned my camera. During the early years of raising Nick and Annie, I found a creative outlet in documenting their childhoods through the lens, capturing on film the joyful energy and mischievous spirit I found in their eyes. With a camera always in hand, I soon found myself in the role of unofficial chronicler for family and friends.

During the Eighties, my husband's job often took us on location for months at a time, frequently to the West Coast where I was able to visit Dad and his wife. In 1989, we officially relocated to Los Angeles (a one-year plan that stretched into several), but by then, Dad had developed Alzheimer's. His jovial humor was fading, and his embraces became increasingly listless. And yet, even in the end when words failed him, I could still find a familiar warmth and recognition in his gaze.

It is now over two decades since that day on the interstate, the day this book was conceived. I had been taking classes and doing portraiture for several years, and at that particular time I was in search of a subject for a series. I had an epiphany during that long drive: I would create an homage to my dad by photographing fathers and daughters. I would capture them in images recalling the black and white photography of the mid-century photojournalists whom I loved in my youth. I began seeking out subjects in family and friends, then friends of friends, always looking for those magical, fleeting moments between fathers and daughters.

The nomadic life I shared with my husband and his work sometimes took us to places with unexpected opportunities to photograph. A portable hand-held camera, first a 35 mm Nikkormat, then a medium format Mamiya, was the perfect vehicle for close, intimate portraits of the people I met. Families chose the locations for photo shoots, introducing interesting challenges for finding the right light to work in (available light being my preference over artificial light). The most rewarding part of each shoot, though, was watching fathers interact with their daughters and discovering the look in their eyes as they basked in each other's company. Through these families I found a road that led back to a time of childhood bliss with a father I adored.

TERRY CORRAO, April, 2016

BRUCE and ELIZABETH STRATTON
Contractor
South Pasadena, California   1991

JACQUES and ADRIANA BOULANGER
Wine Writer // Student
Dover Plains, New York   1997

GREG and GRETA McGEE
Fitness Trainer
New York City   2001

FABRIZIO, MARTA, MATILDE, and EMMA FERRI
Photographer // Student
New York City   2001

J. and ZELDA GROVE
Story/Script Analyst
Frazier Park, Californian   1994

ALAN, TONI, and CHASE OLSTEIN
Vice President, New York food broker
New York City   1998

CRAIG and NELL McKAY
Film Editor
New York City   1994

"There are
moments
when a
glance,
a smile,
the placement of
a hand,
the inclination of
a body,
seem to open up a
window
onto the
mystery
of the
relationship."

Lloyd Fonvielle

ANGELO and ANNEMARIE CORRAO
Film Editor // Student
Los Angeles, California   1995

DORIAN "DOC" and NAVAH PASKOWITZ
Physician and Founder of Paskowitz Surf Camp // Model and Actress
San Onofre, California   1998

RONNIE and EMMA ROOSE
Film Editor
Santa Monica, California   1994

NIGEL and REBECCA PINK
Coach and Fitness Trainer
Millbrook, New York   1998

DAGAN and ISLA ALLARDYCE
Industrial Hygienist
Waterbury Center, Vermont   2014

RICARDO and STEFANIE CARABAJO
Bolivian Parade Participants, Hispanic Day Parade
New York City   2006

MAX MANDELL and BARBARA ROWE
with the Nursery School and Kindergarten Students of the Mandell School
Educator and Founder of Mandell School // Educator and Head of School
New York City   1998

PATRICK and SARA CAVANAUGH
Digital Imaging Specialist, *Rolling Stone* Magazine // Student
Hastings-on-Hudson, New York   1998

SIMON and KEATON MARRIAN
Smoked Fish Purveyor // Student
Westbrookville, New York   1994

LARRY and JULIANNA CLARK
Photographer and Filmmaker // Student
New York City   1999

ROBERT and JENNY MORGENTHAU
Manhattan District Attorney // Executive Director, Fresh Air Fund
New York City   1998

"How many more
times will you remember a certain
afternoon of your childhood, an afternoon that
is so deeply a part of your being that you can't even conceive
of your life without it? Perhaps four, five times more, perhaps not even that.
How many more times will you watch the full moon rise?
Perhaps twenty. And yet it all seems limitless."

Paul Bowles, *The Sheltering Sky*

MOSES and QUINN PENDLETON
Artistic Director, MOMIX Dance Theater
Washington, Connecticut   1994

PETER and McKENNA JOHNSON
Model and Actor
Hastings-on-Hudson, New York   2002

PIETER, KIM, and JULIE KROONENBURG
Film Producer // Wardrobe Assistant // Lion Cub Wrangler
On the film set of *To Walk With Lions*,
Shaba Reserve, Kenya   1998

ROBERT and PEYTON FLOYD
Architect // Student, University of California at Santa Cruz
Austin, Texas   1999

ALLAN and CAITLIN FLAHERTY
Computer Consultant // Student
Los Angeles, California   1994

DAVID and AUSTIN IRVING
Film Professor, New York University // Student
New York City   2001

CHEFS ALAIN LEVY and LEA COLE
Professor of Baking and Pastry, Culinary Institute of America // Alumna, Culinary Institute of America
Hyde Park, New York   2002

RON and ERIKA COHEN
Retired Welder // Actress
Farmer's Market, Los Angeles, California   1994

SIDNEY KUPERSMITH and CAROL ROSENZIEG
Retired Master Plumber // Television Writer and Cancer Activist
Ventura, California   1994

DANIEL and REBECCA JODET
Sculptor // Student
Paris   1997

ROBERT and JOANNA LEVINE
Attorney and Literary Agent
New York City   1994

WALTER and NINA ROSENBLUM
Photographer // Filmmaker
New York City   1998

PRINCE ALEXANDER, DARIA, and FRANCESCA FARMAN-FARMAIAN
Portfolio Manager and Investor
Dutchess County, New York   2006

JEAN-LOUIS, CATHERINE, and CAROLINE TIRRAN
Physical Therapist and Osteopath // Student, La Sorbonne // Fashion Editor
La Baule, Brittany, France   1996

DINO DE LAURENTIIS with, *clockwise from left*,
RAFFAELLA, FRANCESCA, VERONICA, CAROLINA, and DINA DE LAURENTIIS
Film Producer // Film Producer // Film Producer // Actress and Author
Beverly Hills, California   1997

GEORGE and VERSHONYA ARCHIBALD
Proprietor // Manager, Archibald's Bar-B-Que
Northport, Alabama   2013

MARK ROGGEMANN and JAYNE KOONCE
Computer Consultant // Student, Collin College
Plano, Texas   1996

PAUL and JENNIFER WINTER
Anesthesiologist
The Great Hudson Valley Balloon Race, Wappinger Falls, New York   1998

MORRIS and MARY ENGEL
Photographer and Filmmaker // Photo Archivist
New York City   1994

HARVEY WALDMAN and MINONA HEAVILAND
Unit Production Manager for Motion Pictures // Student, Wesleyan University
New York City 1996

MARSHALL VI and CHLOE FIELD
Horse Trainer
Dutchess County, New York   1997

JAMES and HOLLY LAND
Economist and Publisher // Co-Owner, kitchen and bath company
New York City   1998

HAMILTON V, SOPHIA, and ELIZA FISH
Publisher
Garrison, New York   2001

PHILIP and ELIZABETH CORRAO
Human Resources Specialist, United States Postal Service // Student
Queens, New York   1994

LEONARD and KRISTEN GARCIA
Oil and Gas Landman // Student
Austin, Texas   1996

WILLIAM and ELIZABETH MATTES
Advertising Executive // Student
Berkshire School, Sheffield, Massachusetts   1998

LEON and CLARA BOTSTEIN
President, Bard College and Symphony Conductor // Student
Annandale-on-Hudson, New York   1998

HAMILTON and MARGARET MESERVE
County Legislator, Dutchess County, New York // Lecturer, Princeton University
Millbrook, New York   2001

AL HIRSCHFELD and NINA WEST
Caricaturist, *New York Times* // Pianist
New York City   1997

CORKY SMITH and LISA MARIE
Organic Farmer // Actress and Model
Premiere of Tim Burton's *Sleepy Hollow*,
Hollywood, California   1999

MICHEL and EMILIE JEAN
with, *on left*, Marc Minet
Restauranteur // Student // Restaurant Manager
Bastille Day, New York City   1998

MARTIN and JULIET LANDAU
Actor // Actress
Premiere of Tim Burton's *Sleepy Hollow*, Hollywood, California   1999

GUILLAUME, CAPUCINE, and ANAIS TOUTON
Wine Importer
Dover Plaines, New York   1999

CHRIS and CHARLOTTE POTH
Agent for Real Estate Tax Credits
New Canaan, Connecticut   1998

SIR JOHN and SUSANNAH BARRAN
British Civil Servant // Debutante
Rose Ball, London   1999

HOLLAND CONRAD and SYDNEY CONRAD SHAPIRO
Electromechanical Engineer // Costume Supervisor
Wilmington, North Carolina   1995

JAMES, KATHERINE, ELLIE, MAGGIE BURROWS and PARIS SELLON
TV Director // Students
Bel-Air, California   2002

COMMENTARY

CARLOS and ANALIS SOCA   *page ii*
Wolcott, Connecticut, 1996
Carlos was a young schoolboy when I moved into his New York City apartment building as a
new bride in 1974. I watched him grow up and graduate Trinity School and Amherst College,
excelling in academics and athletics. During his high school years, my kids would beg for him
to babysit because he did the coolest things with them. Carlos' family became our family, and
his mother often invited us to dinners where we devoured her Cuban roast pork. In this photograph, Carlos holds his infant daughter Analis, who was being christened in an old white
clapboard Connecticut church.

J.B., EMMA, MARY, and ISABEL WHITE   *page viii*
Ojai, California, 1994
This is the first photograph I shot for the book. J.B. and his family had recently
moved from New Jersey to California so he could pursue a career in screenwriting.
The family was still settling into their new environment and recovering from the
recent Northridge earthquake. It was a Saturday afternoon and Emma (eleven),
Mary (nine) and Isabel (six) were returning from practice and a birthday party. As
they gathered together on the curb outside their house, J.B. took a quiet moment to
bask in the warmth of his girls' company.

BRUCE and ELIZABETH STRATTON   *page 5*
South Pasadena, California, 1991

In July of 1999, my cousin Connie and her husband Bruce were visiting Hawaii where they joined thousands of solar chasers awaiting a rare total eclipse of the sun. They had taken a beeper with them because they were expecting the birth of their adopted baby in a couple of weeks. Upon returning to the Los Angeles airport, the beeper sounded and they found out that they had just become parents! They rushed to the hospital to meet their new daughter Elizabeth Olga, just hours old. A few days later, I visited their home in South Pasadena to meet the recent addition to the family and take some photographs. Though this portrait was taken a few years before my father-daughter project was initiated, it seemed a perfect addition.

JACQUES and ADRIANA BOULANGER   *page 7*
Dover Plains, New York, 1997

During the 1990s, my family and I rented a farmhouse—formerly an 1800s toll house—on the Boulangers' farm in Dutchess County, New York. On weekends, when Jacques would come up with his family, I enjoyed lengthy conversations with him as he tended to his collection of vintage sports cars. One day I saw some activity out on the driveway. Jacques was giving his teenage daughter Adriana a driving lesson in his 1968 Austin Healy BJ8. He tried to remain calm and reassuring in spite of the fact that Adriana was attempting to handle the clutch in her clogs.

GREG and GRETA McGEE   *page 8*
New York City, 2001

Greg, a New York City fitness trainer, was home with his daughter Greta while her mom Fulvia was working on a photo shoot. As a makeup artist, Fulvia would frequently travel abroad for work. Greg and Greta would hold down the fort, often pass afternoons playing on Greg's gym equipment together. Greta loved showing off her baby muscles by wrapping her arms around her dad's neck as he did chin-ups.

FABRIZIO, MARTA, MATILDE, and EMMA FERRI *page 9*
New York City, 2001

Fabrizio and the beautiful ballerina Alessandra Ferri were in New York with daughters Marta, Matilde, and baby Emma for the Christmas holidays. This photograph was taken in their West Side apartment, just weeks after the birth of Emma. The afternoon sun reflected off the Hudson River and filled the room with a warm light. Weeks later, when Fabrizio saw the photographs, he took them in quietly. Then, smiling, he remarked that it was the first time he truly saw himself as the father of not just two, but three daughters.

J. and ZELDA GROVE *page 11*
Frazier Park, California, 1994

A week prior to taking this photograph, I spent a long night in the hospital birthing room with Zelda's mom Dana, awaiting Zelda's birth. Over the course of the night, I shot rolls of film, but nothing compared to this moment at the family's mountain cabin when J. held his newborn daughter, and Cody the dog realized he was no longer an only child.

ALAN, TONI, and CHASE OLSTEIN *page 12*
New York City, 1998

I spotted the Olsteins at the Bastille Day celebrations outside Provence restaurant in Soho; Dad was juggling both his girls while Mom stepped away for a moment. In spite of the heat and crowds, they kindly paused and let me take their photograph. It was a classic father-daughter moment, captured shortly before the inevitable meltdown.

CRAIG and NELL McKAY *page 13*
New York City, 1994

One night, my husband and I arrived for dinner at Craig and Patsy McKay's apartment just as they were finishing Nell's nightly ritual of a bath and a bedtime story. All scrubbed and combed, Nell curled up with Craig in their favorite armchair to read *The Wind in the Willows*. Swept into a faraway land, Nell was oblivious to the nighttime cacophony of mid-Manhattan sirens and taxi horns outside her window.

ANGELO and ANNEMARIE CORRAO *page 15*

Los Angeles, California, 1995

My husband and our thirteen-year-old daughter Annie stood backstage waiting for her cue. It was her ballet studio's year-end performance of *Four Seasons*. Angelo has always shared his love of the arts with our children, and cheered on Annie's passion for dance. Not long after this was taken we moved back East, where at her new school in the Berkshires she left dancing behind and discovered lacrosse, field hockey, and boys.

DORIAN "DOC" and NAVAH PASKOWITZ *pages 16, 17*

San Onofre, California, 1998

At the Paskowitz Surf Camp, one escapes the stresses of city life, plunging into days spent waiting for the big waves, enjoying delicious barbecues on the beach, engaging in philosophical conversations with Doc, and stealing siestas under the umbrella. Doc was thrilled to have a portrait taken with his daughter Navah. He said it was the first time anyone asked for just the two of them (rather than his eight sons). Before leaving camp, Doc sent me on my way with an autographed copy of his inspiring book *Surfing and Health*.

RONNIE and EMMA ROOSE *page 18*

Santa Monica, California, 1994

Ronnie, a longtime New York friend and film colleague of my husband, moved to California with his family about the same time that we did. During our shared time in Los Angeles, we often got together at the Rooses' home for afternoons of good food and ongoing discussions about film and photography. Emma had just celebrated her fourth birthday and the backyard was filled with new toys and a shiny new bicycle with training wheels, but ultimately nothing could beat a joyous romp on her dad's back.

NIGEL and REBECCA PINK   *page 19*
Millbrook, New York, 1998

Nigel and his family moved from England to Millbrook during the mid-90s, and his two daughters Rebecca and Charlotte quickly became Americanized, much to his chagrin. One day they came to my house for lunch, and I asked if they would mind if I took a few snapshots so I could try out a new camera. Nigel, a soccer coach, brought out a ball for some scrimmaging shots with his daughters. A wonderful moment came afterward, when I found Nigel and Rebecca in a playful whirl around the lawn, Rebecca squealing in delight.

DAGAN and ISLA ALLARDYCE   *page 21*
Waterbury Center, Vermont, 2014

One aspect of taking twenty years to complete a project is that one grows old— maybe even old enough to have a grandchild. And so I have. My daughter Annie and her husband Dagan now have a daughter named Isla Anne. Dagan, who has a love of all things with motors and gears, has introduced Isla to a mechanical world. Her eyes twinkle with joy when she sets off on an adventure with her dad. In the winter, they do laps around the house on the snowmobile. When summer arrives, they are on the lawn tractor in the early morning, then off in the pickup truck to the dump and hardware store, followed by a stop for a breakfast sandwich. Later in the afternoon it's down to the beaver creek, looking for crawfish, tadpoles, and snails. Life with dad is going to be an adventure for this little girl.

RICARDO and STEFANIE CARABAJO   *page 22*
New York City, 2006

During the Hispanic Day Parade in Manhattan, I spotted Ricardo and his daughter Stefanie in vibrant costumes standing among their fellow Bolivian marchers. They had just completed the Fifth Avenue parade route and were gathering on one of the side streets of the Upper East Side. Stefanie, tired from marching, snuggled into her dad's arms.

MAX MANDELL and BARBARA ROWE   *page 23*
New York City, 1998

An early education pioneer, Max founded Mandell Nursery School and Kindergarten in 1939. He and his daughter Barbara Rowe ran the school for many years, and his granddaughter Gabriella Rowe continued the legacy. I met the family when my own children attended the Mandell School in the early 80s, and we have remained friends ever since. I will always remember Max standing outside every morning in jacket and tie, holding out his arms to greet the children as they came running to him. Here, Max and Barbara sit among a group of nursery school and kindergarten students on the stoop of their brownstone school. (The children, in alphabetical order, are Emily Brigstocke; Oliver di Costanzo; Derek Cuevas; Jessica Hirschorn; Julia Kieserman; Kate Levien; Zachary Mittman; Jamie Rappaport; Carolyn Scheinberg; Ariana Silvan-Gray; Sam Sternberg; and Lee Zee.)

PATRICK and SARA CAVANAUGH   *page 24*
Hastings-on-Hudson, New York, 1998

Patrick has worked for *Rolling Stone* magazine for more than 25 years and says he will proudly retire as one of the magazine's longest employed hippies. I adored Patrick from the moment I met him at the Marrians' annual croquet party. When I went to their home, Sara and Patrick played basketball in the driveway for hours. Their dog loved being part of every family activity, including photo-ops.

SIMON and KEATON MARRIAN   *page 25*
Westbrookville, New York, 1994

Simon grew up in Kenya and England and returned to Africa as a young man to lead safaris in the Sudan. As a hobby, he taught himself to smoke locally caught tuna, which he sold to upscale safari lodges. Eventually, Simon moved to the United States with his American wife Libba and their two children, where he launched a successful smoked fish business. Every summer, the family hosts the Marrian Cup croquet party for their friends. During the annual party setup, Keaton and Simon paused long enough to have a picture taken with Koko, Libba's toy gorilla from FAO Schwartz, named after the real-life gorilla who learned American Sign Language.

LARRY and JULIANNA CLARK   *page 26*

New York City, 1999

Arriving for the first time at Larry Clark's Tribeca loft, I was confronted by his tower of skateboards stacked inside the front door. It was going to be interesting meeting this edgy artist, known for his controversial photography books (*Tulsa, Teenage Lust*) and films (*Kids, Bully*) and seeing him firsthand in his role as a father. I accompanied him to Penn Station to meet his daughter and son, who were coming from their mom's house in New Jersey for a weekend in the city. It became apparent right away that the children adored their father—and he them—as we emerged from the underground station. Oblivious to the rush hour chaos on Seventh Avenue, Juliana and her father shared a hug before hailing a cab to go see a performance of *Fuerza Bruta*.

ROBERT and JENNY MORGENTHAU   *page 27*

New York City, 1998

Robert and Jenny Morgenthau are a remarkable father and daughter pair. As the Manhattan District Attorney, Morgenthau worked for decades as a tireless advocate for justice. (In fact, the *Law and Order* District Attorney Adam Schiff is based on Morgenthau.) Jenny Morgenthau is the executive director of the Fresh Air Fund, which provides free summer vacations for thousands of inner-city kids. Taking an afternoon break from their demanding schedules, they enjoyed a walk near the court houses of Lower Manhattan.

MOSES and QUINN PENDLETON   *page 29*

Washington, Connecticut, 1994

I arrived to Moses Pendleton's MOMIX dance studios with a van full of the company's New York City dancers who had come to rehearse for a tour in Spain. Upon arrival, Moses apologized that he would need to work with them for several hours before we could do the scheduled shoot, affording me the opportunity to watch this remarkably talented choreographer in action. Later that afternoon, we drove to a nearby lake where Moses swims every day, and he and Quinn performed some of their favorite acrobatics in the water.

PETER and McKENNA JOHNSON *page 31*

Hastings-on-Hudson, New York, 2002

I was introduced to Peter Johnson, the lead actor in Bruce Weber's film *Chop Suey*, by my husband who was the film's editor. Weber had discovered then-fifteen-year-old Peter at Dan Gables' Wrestling Camp at the University of Iowa, where Weber was doing a photo shoot. It was exciting to have the opportunity to photograph Peter after witnessing his willingness to give himself completely to the camera in *Chop Suey*. During our shoot along the Hudson River, he said that he suspected he would be the youngest dad in the book—he was eighteen years old when McKenna was born.

PIETER, JULIE, and KIM KROONENBERG *pages 32, 33*

Shaba Reserve, Kenya, 1998

Pieter's film production company was in Kenya filming *To Walk With Lions*, a sequel to *Born Free*. His crew included his two daughters: Kim was beginning her career in film production, and Julie had a degree in exotic animal training. My husband was editing the film, so he and I joined the crew for a brief time on location. Once on the set, we discovered the production had imported seven Californian lions to Africa for the film. The local lions apparently were not prepared to perform for the camera. Early on the morning of our last day in Shaba, we were able to arrange a photo shoot and drove the 45 minutes through the African bush to the movie set. The cub was in a rambunctious mood and Julie, the lion cub wrangler, had to coax the young one into sitting by tossing large chunks of raw meat its way.

ROBERT and PEYTON FLOYD *page 34*

Austin, Texas, 1999

Those who met Peyton will never forget this beautiful and extraordinarily talented young woman. I photographed her and her dad Robert at their Austin home perched high above a ravine. Peyton, an accomplished dancer, jumped up on the deck railing without a moment's hesitation and walked its length with assured gracefulness. It was a joy watching her and her father interact; their resemblance was remarkable, their camaraderie lighthearted. A year later, a tragic incident would occur; Peyton would die in a car accident coming home from New York. Peyton's mother Robbie Davis-Floyd told me recently, "Peyton was a dreamer, always reaching for the sky. Robert gave her the solid ground she walked upon and passed on his physical giftedness to her as well, which is why she was such an amazing dancer… Now she lives in the sky she was always reaching for, and perhaps her dad, who has also passed on, dances with her there."

ALLAN and KAITY FLAHERTY *page 35*

Los Angeles, California, 1994

Kaity and my daughter Annie danced together several days a week in ballet class when we lived in Los Angeles. Kaity always had excellent form and great flexibility. This shot was taken during a weekend visit to her dad's apartment where, up on the roof, Allan proved to have equally good form.

DAVID and AUSTIN IRVING *page 36*

New York City, 2001

I began photographing Austin when she was nine years old, and here at eighteen, she was in the midst of applying to college. She was rushing to finish her photography portfolio to meet the deadline for submission that afternoon. David, a professor, was well versed in the college application process and lent his expert opinion in Austin's selection.

ALAIN LEVY and LEA COLE *page 37*

Hyde Park, New York, 2002

Chef Levy is a legendary pastry instructor at the Culinary Institute of America. His daughter Lea Cole graduated from CIA as well, and when I met her, she was working with my son at Follow Production, a television production company which creates shows for the Food Network. Lea got back into her chef's jacket and into the pastry kitchen at CIA for this portrait with her dad.

RON and ERIKA COHEN *page 38*

Los Angeles, California, 1994

Erika was part of my extended family of ex-New Yorkers living in Los Angeles. She had come to California to pursue her career in acting, and on this afternoon we met up with her father, who was visiting from Toronto. This photo captures a moment when Erika and Ron were browsing the market stalls for souvenirs. They bantered over which trinket to buy (Erika didn't share her dad's taste in key chains). I think all daughters derive great pleasure in tormenting their dads from time to time.

SIDNEY KUPERSMITH and CAROL ROSENSWEIG   *page 39*
Ventura, California, 1994
Sidney moved to a retirement home in Ventura after his wife of 60 years died, and every week his daughter Carol would drive up from Beverly Hills to visit. Carol shared with me that in his youth, Sidney played the organ for silent movies. She lovingly referred to her dapper dad as a strong-willed "Charles in Charge," even into his nineties. But ever since childhood, Carol always found a way to brighten up his days with her humor and charismatic personality.

DANIEL and REBECCA JODET   *page 41*
Paris, 1997
Daniel was showing his sculptures at the Paris Trans Art '97 exhibition where I was debuting a few of my father-daughter photographs. Here, Rebecca and Daniel stand next to his life-size horse sculpture, she in her gothic black velvet dress and he with chisel in hand.

ROBERT and JOANNA LEVINE   *page 42*
New York City, 1994
Bob Levine, an entertainment lawyer and literary agent in Manhattan, enjoyed the short walk from the office to his home on Central Park West, where his daughter Joanna eagerly awaited his arrival. After a visit to the park playground across the street, they shared a few quiet minutes in the living room before dinner.

WALTER and NINA ROSENBLUM   *page 43*
Queens, New York, 1998
Walter, a noted photographer and educator, was president of the Photo League in the 1940s and a war photographer who captured iconic images of the Normandy landing. After the war, he married Naomi Rosenblum, author of *A World History of Photography.* Their daughter Nina, growing up in her family's artistic community, became an Oscar-nominated documentary film-maker and in 2012 made *Ordinary Miracles,* a documentary about the Photo League. Together at Walter's studio in Long Island City, they talked about their passion for imagery and storytelling.

PRINCE ALEXANDER, DARIA, and FRANCESCA FARMAN-FARMAIAN *page 44*

Dutchess County, New York, 2006

It was a crisp autumn day and there was a blustery wind outside the family's country house. Baby Francesca was just beginning to walk and her father was worried the strong gusts could knock her down. Big sister Daria took Francesca's hand and coaxed her up the winding road with them. Back at the house, the girls' mother Patricia and their two brothers kept hot chocolate waiting for our return. Hanging out with the family in the kitchen, I listened to them converse in both Spanish and English. Alexander told me he spent much of his youth in Venezuela (his father, a descendant of the Persian Qajar dynasty, was Iran's first ambassador there) and wanted to give his children the gift of being bilingual as well.

JEAN LOUIS, CAROLINE, and CATHERINE TIRRAN *page 45*

La Baule, Brittany, France, 1996

While visiting my friend Caroline in Paris, she invited me to her hometown of La Baule on the Brittany coast. We went to visit her parents and her sister Catherine, who was home on summer break from La Sorbonne. Jean Louis offered to take everyone down to Chez Mignon along the harbor for one of the famed *gaufres*, a cream-drenched waffle covered with a silky chocolate spread. After the decadent treat, father and daughters agreed that a walk on the white sand beach was in order.

DINO, FRANCESCA, VERONICA, RAFFAELLA, CAROLYNA, and DINA DE LAURENTIIS *page 47*

Beverly Hills, California, 1997

Dino was at his hilltop residence, not far from Hollywood where he produced many successful feature films. Over the span of his career, he produced classics such as Fellini's *La Strada* and *Nights of Cabiria* and many memorable American films, including *King Kong, Barbarella, Serpico,* and *Blue Velvet*. Joining him for lunch were his wife Martha and his five daughters: Francesca, Veronica, and Raffaella (from Dino's first marriage to Italian movie star Silvana Mangano), and Carolyna and Dina (his daughters with wife and co-producer Martha). Dino tore himself away from his much-loved Italian soccer broadcast to pass through the kitchen and confer with his Italian chef Gigi about the pasta sauce for lunch, then stepped into the garden to help orchestrate the family photo shoot. He relished every minute of being in the midst of his five girls.

GEORGE and VERSHONYA ARCHIBALD *page 48*
Northport, Alabama, 2013

It was peak time for barbecue pickup at Archibald's, a small cinderblock rib shack that turns out some of the best barbecue in Alabama. Mr. Archibald has been overseeing the pit and the carving since he took over his dad's business, which was founded in 1962. I asked Mr. Archibald if his daughter will take over when he retires and he said probably not; it's his 23-year-old granddaughter who is most interested in running the family business. Things were getting hectic and crowds were lining up during our shoot, but we managed to clear the room and capture a few shots of Mr. Archibald and Vershonya serving up their famous rib sandwich.

MARK ROGGEMANN and JAYNE KOONCE *page 49*
Plano, Texas, 1996

As a young girl, my niece Jayne enjoyed racing remote-controlled cars with her stepfather Mark, but during her teen years, go-kart racing became their shared passion. Mark was an experienced Laydown Enduro Go-Kart racer, and he taught Jayne everything he knew, from changing tires to jumpstarting engines. At an indoor track in Dallas, Mark's driving skills on the course were smooth and precise, following the line and acing every corner, but Jayne's competitive spirit often found her overtaking him on the outside and racing flat out to the finish.

PAUL and JENNIFER WINTER *page 51*
Dutchess County, New York, 1998

Balloonists Paul and twelve-year-old Jennifer were doing a demonstration at the Great Hudson Valley Balloon Race in Wappinger Falls, NY. They had partially inflated an old grounded balloon and released inside it a half-balloon, which visitors were invited to raise and lower with a remote control. After a long day, the strong rays of the setting sun cut through the balloon opening just enough to cast distorted shadows of Paul and Jennifer on the nylon wall.

MORRIS and MARY ENGEL *page 52*

New York City, 1994

Mary and I have been close friends ever since she moved into our apartment building on the Upper West Side in Manhattan in the late 80s. She is the daughter of two of my most admired photographers and filmmakers, Morris Engel and Ruth Orkin. She also acts as the archivist for their work. In this shot, Mary and Morris lean through the window of their apartment building on Central Park West, the same one through which Ruth took the iconic photographs in her book *A World Through My Window.*

HARVEY WALDMAN and MINONA HEAVILAND *page 53*

New York City, 1996

During a visit home from college, Minona challenged her father to a game of chess. Harvey brought out his favorite board with its beautifully carved pieces, and they sat by the window in the living room overlooking West 88th Street and Broadway. The room brought back many happy memories for me. It was always a special place, a big rambling apartment where our merry band of friends would meet up for dinners, celebrations, and intimate evenings. Minona and Harvey seemed equally content in their contemplative world, quietly sharing each other's company.

MARSHALL VI and CHLOE FIELD *page 54*

Dutchess County, New York, 1997

On his farm north of New York City, Marshall plants crop plots to attract many species of wildlife looking for food, shelter, and nesting. Marshall, who comes from a long line of avid outdoorsmen, scooped up four-year-old Chloe for their ritual evening safari, binoculars in hand. After crossing rugged paths, wooded hills and open fields, Marshall stopped the ATV to let Chloe explore aqua critters in the clear water of Wappinger Creek.

JAMES and HOLLY LAND   *page 55*
New York City, 1998
Jim and his wife Nancy live on the family cattle ranch in East Texas from where they run their publishing services business. For several years they kept an apartment in New York, which is where I met them. Their daughter Holly had come from Delaware to visit for the Christmas holidays. Dashing around town doing last-minute shopping, Jim and Holly stopped at a kiosk in Central Park for an afternoon cup of coffee. Jim enjoyed teasing Holly, saying she had two religions: the religion of Buddha and the religion of Gucci.

HAMILTON V, SOPHIA, and ELIZA FISH   *page 56*
Garrison, New York, 2001
Hamilton, the descendent of four generations of prominent New York statesmen and politicians, took his daughters to visit the family's ancestral gravesite at St. Philip's Church-in-the-Highlands Cemetery in Garrison. After paying their respects to Hamilton Fish I, II, III, and IV, they wandered down to their favorite spot along the Hudson River for some play time across from majestic West Point.

PHILIP and ELIZABETH CORRAO   *page 57*
Queens, New York, 1994
On a warm summer afternoon, I joined my brother-in-law Phil and his daughter Elizabeth for an Italian Sunday supper in the backyard of my in-laws' home. A kind and devoted dad, Phil has stood by his daughter since the moment she came into the world, two months premature. Elizabeth now teaches fourth grade in the Bronx, and she's a wife and mother of two little girls on whom Phil dotes with equal devotion.

LEONARD and KRISTEN GARCIA   *page 58*

Austin, Texas, 1996

My niece Kristen, a senior on the Westwood High School Sundancer drill team, and her dad Leonard, a Texas oil and gas landman, paused during rehearsal for their Homecoming Week performance. For weeks prior, the forty Sundancers had been teaching their dads a three-minute dance routine (excluding high kicks), which the fathers and daughters would perform for the half-time show at the Homecoming football game. Leonard believes he did not embarrass Kristen too much.

WILLIAM and ELIZABETH MATTES   *page 59*

Sheffield, Massachusetts, 1998

Elizabeth and my daughter Annie became fast friends their freshman year at Berkshire School and have remained close to this day. This shot was taken during Parents' Weekend, when students showed off their prowess on the athletic fields. Elizabeth had just injured her ankle in a lacrosse game and had to be sidelined. Knowing his daughter was upset at not playing, Bill reassuringly stood by, lending good cheer to both her and the team.

LEON and CLARA BOTSTEIN   *page 61*

Annandale-on-Hudson, New York, 1998

I became acquainted with college president and symphony conductor Leon Botstein during the late 90s when my son attended Bard College. We met personally during a signing of his book *Jefferson's Children* in nearby Millbrook. The next month, he invited me for a photo shoot at the President's House, his home on the Bard campus. An imposing figure, Leon has a larger-than-life presence. But when Clara came down the stairs with her violin in hand, I watched his eyes light up—like so many fathers, he immediately softened in the presence of his daughter. Leon also proved to be experienced in front of the camera and helped coach his twelve-year-old daughter in her poses.

HAMILTON and MARGARET MESERVE   *page 62*

Millbrook, New York, 2001

When I met Ham and his wife Helen for the first time, I mentioned to Helen that I was a photographer and that I thought Ham had a great profile. Chuckling, she said, "Well, you know who his mother is, don't you? Margaret Hamilton, The Wicked Witch of the West!" A few weeks later, I was able to capture all three generations in profile: Ham and his daughter Margaret with an Al Hirschfeld caricature of Margaret Hamilton in the 1977 Broadway play, *The Three Sisters.*

AL HIRSCHFELD and NINA WEST   *page 63*

New York City, 1997

When Nina was a newborn, Al Hirschfeld, the famed caricaturist for the *New York Times,* started hiding Nina's name in his drawings in the Arts section as a treasure hunt for his friends. It wasn't long before word got out, and it became a Sunday ritual for children and adults alike to search for the NINAs in celebrities' sideburns and sleeves. Now an adult, Nina lives in Texas and comes home to New York City for frequent visits. It was a rare opportunity to finally meet the elusive Nina, whom so many of us had tried to find every week in the paper. A classically trained pianist, she and Al posed in his brownstone parlor, framed by Al's wall of caricatures.

LISA MARIE and CORKY SMITH   *pages 64, 65*

Hollywood, California, 1999

Model and actress Lisa Marie was at the premiere of Tim Burton's *Sleepy Hollow* at Grauman's Chinese Theater. She played the role of Ichabod Crane's mother in the film, her third collaboration with director and then-fiancé Tim Burton. Lisa Marie's dad Corky had flown in from New Jersey to see his daughter's performance. Lisa Marie and I plotted a surprise attack on her camera-shy dad with this photo op on the red carpet.

MICHEL and EMILIE JEAN   *page 66*

New York City, 1998

Every July 14, Michel and Patricia Jean gave one of the best Bastille Day parties in New York City. Their Soho restaurant Provence would co-host a daylong tournament of *petanque* on McDougal Street. But it was during the evening festivities that things got interesting. At the restaurant, with "La Marseillaise" blaring, Michel and his staff would toast each table with a waving French flag and the sabering of champagne bottles. Bubbles overflowed from high-held flutes. By midnight, all inhibitions had vanished and revelers danced on the tabletops until the wee hours. Emilie Jean has the mixed blessing of having been born on Bastille Day. In this photograph, she was celebrating her Sweet Six-teen with a hug from Dad and kiss from the restaurant manager, Marc Minet.

MARTIN and JULIET LANDAU   *page 67*

Hollywood, California, 1999

In November, 1999, Tim Burton's *Sleepy Hollow* premiered at Grauman's Chinese Theater on Hollywood Boulevard. Actor Martin Landau, who had a cameo in the opening sequence of the film (a memorable beheading scene), attended the open-ing with his daughter Juliet. I found them celebrating at the after-party in the for-mer Convent of the Immaculate Heart, enjoying a drink together in the medieval dining hall. Both father and daughter had previously worked together on another Burton film, *Ed Wood*—Juliet as Loretta King and Martin in his Oscar-winning performance as Bela Lugosi.

GUILLAUME, CAPUCINE, and ANAIS TOUTON   *page 68*

Dutchess County, New York, 1999

Guillaume and his family were guests at a James Bond-themed party at Jacques and Carol Boulanger's country home in Dutchess County. Everyone came in costume from the Bond films; Guillaume came as a big heart "because James Bond was always falling in love." While we dined under the arbor and apple trees, partaking of the exceptional food and wine, Capu-cine and her little sister Anais kept trying to jump in the pool, keeping their parents very busy.

CHRIS and CHARLOTTE POTH *page 69*
New Canaan, Connecticut, 1998
It was Halloween night when a friend and I dropped by the Poths' house for a visit. Their daughter Charlotte hadn't finished her costume yet, so we all pitched in, wrangling yards of muslin to get her wrapped up as a princess mummy. I borrowed the family camera to grab a photo of father and daughter before they left for trick-or-treating.

SIR JOHN and SUSANNAH BARRAN *page 70*
London, 1999
Early April to August marks "The London Season" when young women make their debut into society. Sir John "Pony" Barran and his debutante daughter Susi were attending the Rose Ball, one of the Season's highlights. Sir John's wife Lady Jane Barran was co-chairing the event and extended an invitation to come photograph the debutantes and their fathers dancing at the Ball.

HOLLAND CONRAD and SIDNEY CONRAD SHAPIRO *page 71*
Wilmington, North Carolina, 1995
Sidney returned to her childhood home in North Carolina for her wedding to Scott Shapiro, whom she had met while working in Los Angeles. Two hours prior to the ceremony, a hurricane-force rainstorm drenched Wilmington, almost forcing the outdoor wedding at Airlie Gardens to be moved indoors. But the sun came out in time, allowing Holland to escort his daughter down the green path. This photo seems to capture some of the ineffable emotions that father and daughter feel on such a big day.

JAMES, KATHERINE, ELLIE, MAGGIE BURROWS, and PARIS SELLON *page 72*
Bel-Air, California, 2002
When I arrived at the Burrows home, I was greeted by Jack, an enthusiastic yellow Labrador, and four exuberant girls, all creating a chaotic din in the kitchen. Their dad Jim, the TV director known for his witty hand in *The Big Bang Theory, Will and Grace, Friends,* and *Cheers,* seemed to delight in the commotion. When we headed out to the terraced garden to take

some pictures, Jim suggested using Paris' course of dog jumps for the family photo shoot. His older daughters had been cheerleaders and led everyone in a simultaneous group jump by calling out the countdown. Perfect results on the first roll of film!

ACKNOWLEDGMENTS

Throughout the twenty years of working on this project, I have been met with extraordinary kindness and generosity. It is to these wonderful people I give my heartfelt thanks and deepest appreciation:

Lloyd Fonvielle, for planting the seed to pursue this photo series; Vicki Dwight and Michael Amorous of Chelsea Photographic Services, Jean-Marc Hanon, Silver Lab, and On Location, all of whom contributed beautiful black and white prints; Jeff Hirsch of Fotocare, for all of the TLC; Henry Froelich and Mamiya America, whose generosity made the 645 camera a reality for me; Carrie Hunt, for her creative vision in the initial layout of the book; Emily Conner, for her keen editorial eye; Michele Myatt Quinn, for making the book shine so fine; JillEllyn Riley, for her invaluable editorial advice and unwavering enthusiasm; J.B. White, for his wonderful foreword; and Easty Lambert-Brown, for her expertise, guidance, and humor during the publishing process.

Thanks to Bruce Weber and Nan Bush, for believing in the project from its earliest days; Steven, Shoshana, and Seneca Sebring, for their much-appreciated support; Peter Margonelli, for 35 years of friendship and photographic advice at every step; Richard Vagnon, for championing my work and taking it to exhibition in Paris; Diane Schaub, a.k.a. the Queen of Opinions, for perpetually keeping me in stitches; Mary Engel, for her loyalty, her generosity of spirit, and for making the New York City photography world a little less intimidating. A special acknowledgement to Mary's mother, the late photographer Ruth Orkin. Her early black and white images ignited the passion to cultivate a photojournalist style in my own work.

To dear friends, teachers and colleagues: Lee Rossi; Libba Marrian; Mitch Levine; Carol, Victoria, and Drew Lynford; Camilla Toniolo and Harvey Waldman; Mona Davis and Rafael Cuves; T.J. Girard and Ricardo Galvez; Angela, Jay, and Hugo Pires; Yola Monakhov; Andrew French; Martha DeLaurentiis; Louise Kerz Hirschfeld; Lisa Marie; Tim Burton; Heather McNallie; Fulvia Farolfi; Cherry Vanilla; Pam and Bill Doyle; Kathleen Vuillet; Roland Augustine; Betty Kuhner; Henry Horenstein; Nancy, Jim, and Matthew Land; Ken Cohen and Gabriella Rowe; Vivian Knussi; Kelli Chilton; Caroline Tirran Livingston; Robert Levine; Jeany Wolf; Rick Hibbard; Robert Herman; Chris Cole; Anthony Masina; Carmen Piccini; Kristina Decter; Daphne Howard; Judy Werner; Nina Di Marco; Peter Miller; Felicity Marrian; Diane Rossi; Anne Page Roose; Nancy

Rudolph; Jim Heimann; Matt Lewis; Kate Hays; Christina Frantom; Andrew Grace; Debbie Bond; Chip Brantley; Jeremy Butler; Mary Kerr; Kaitlin Goins; Serena Blount Fortenberry; Scott Fuller; Pete Beatty.

And to my family, to whom I owe everything: Mom and Dad (how much you are missed); our daughter Annie Corrao Allardyce, whose fun-loving relationship with her dad has been a constant source of joy and inspiration; our son-in-law and amazing dad in his own right, Dagan Allardyce; and their adorable, above-average daughter Isla Anne; our son Nick Corrao, for all of his encouragement and support, especially with the tech stuff; and our daughter-in-law Amanda Shaw Corrao, for her artistic talent and infinite patience throughout the design process (plus blessing us with a beautiful grandson, Angelo Teodoro "Theo," in the midst of it all). My deepest love to my extraordinary husband and the father of our children, Angelo Corrao, whose endless support and creative input are beyond the realm of the norm.

A hunk'a love to the other members of my family, all of whom shared in this book's journey: Barbara and Leonard Garcia; Carl John Garcia; Kristen Maxwell; Mandy and Mark Roggemann; Scott Stevenson; Jayne Benne; Jean Stevenson; Maria Corrao; Philip Corrao; Elizabeth Corrao and Matt, Emily, and Sofia Fields; Robbie Davis-Floyd; Peyton and Jason Floyd; Robert, Debbie, and Erin Floyd; Connie, Bruce, and Elizabeth Stratton; Katy Cutter; Carol and Bill Cutter; Laura and Roy Gaut; Charlie Cutter; Swifty and Juliette Stevenson; and Nancy, Dean, Molly, and Henry Grover.

Finally, my profound thanks to the fathers and daughters who appear in these pages. It is their spirit this book celebrates.

MOSES and QUINN PENDLETON
Washington, Connecticut   1994